I kNOw TINY SECRETS

by Latasha Fleming

Illustrated by Colleen Madden

Dear Courageous Parents & Readers,

This book is near and dear to me as I am a survivor of sexual abuse.

I once feared those shameful childhood incidents that shaped me into an adult.
As a child, I had no one to talk to, no one to confide in...
to keep me from harm.

Admittedly, this conversation is not an easy one to have with children
but it is invaluable time spent towards educating them about sexual abuse
and keeping themselves safe.

This is an opportunity to help children help themselves.
Children should be encouraged to speak up in the event of abuse.
My hopes for "Know Tiny Secrets" is that children will come to
"know" the secrets of child sexual abuse, so there will be "no" secrets
between them and a potential abuser.

Whether you are an adult victim of child abuse or know a victim,
talk to children about abuse and how to keep safe.
Establish open communication with children so they will talk
about uncomfortable touches and report incidents immediately.
Pay attention to a child's body language and sudden behavioral changes.

And teach children with love and respect and help them
understand that there are
"Know Tiny Secrets"
when it comes to keeping safe from sexual abuse.

L.F.

This book is for my India Marie
and dedicated to all children
who are victims of abuse,
neglect and uncertainty.

Thank you to Tameria Smith.
You are an awesome friend.

—LF

When you were in mommy's tummy,
you were a tiny little seed.
And then...with love and care,
You grew into a beautiful baby
with

hands, ears and funny little feet.

2

3

Then you turned into an infant,
pointing and grabbing at everything.

And grew bigger.

4

And bigger!

And as you grow...

from an infant
to a toddler...

Crawling, standing, stepping...
making your way into the world...

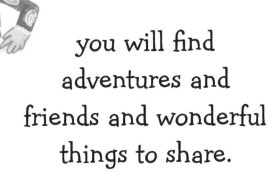

you will find
adventures and
friends and wonderful
things to share.

But did you know that some things
are just for you and you don't have
to share them?

That's right. You don't have to share
the private parts of you.
We all are special and unique and
THAT is pretty cool!

But we all have eyes and ears, elbows
hands and feet.

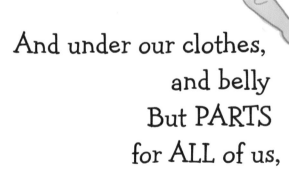 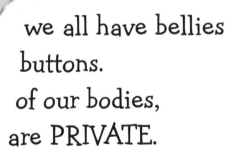

And under our clothes,
and belly
But PARTS
for ALL of us,

we all have bellies
buttons.
of our bodies,
are PRIVATE.

10

PRIVATE FOR A GIRL

Under your
underclothes,
front and back,
is YOUR
PRIVATE
BODY.
Keep it
PRIVATE
and
safe.

PRIVATE FOR A BOY

Under your
underclothes,
front and back,
is YOUR
PRIVATE
BODY.
Keep it
PRIVATE
and
safe.

Your body is special and
wonderful but to keep it SAFE,
keep it PRIVATE.

This means, if someone wants to touch you,
in a private place, you say NO and you TELL
someone you TRUST right away.

ALWAYS SAY NO
to KEEP THE PRIVATE PARTS
OF YOUR BODY SAFE.
Keep your EYES and EARS open for SIGNS
when you are with big people. SIGNS are clues
that someone wants to touch you
in your private places.

If you CAN'T SAY NO to make them stop,
then TELL SOMEONE YOU TRUST RIGHT AWAY.

Sometimes, tickling can be a sign.

Tickling that happens when you don't want it or tickling that changes OR moves from your safe tickle spots to the
PRIVATE PARTS OF YOU
is a sign.

Tell that person to STOP
and go tell someone
you trust right away.

Sometimes, wrestling can be a sign.

Wrestling that happens when you don't want it
or wrestling that
changes from wrestling to touching the
PRIVATE PARTS OF YOU

is a sign.

Tell that person to STOP
and go tell someone
you trust right away.

Big people that want to help you in the bathroom
WHEN YOU DON'T NEED HELP,

is a sign.

Tell that person to GO AWAY
and go tell someone
you trust right away.

22

KNOW

SECRETS

when it comes to your BODY and keeping it
SAFE AND PRIVATE. Big people that LOVE YOU and
RESPECT your PRIVATE BODY, will not try to trick
you or ask you to keep secrets about touching.

TINY
TO KEEP

Big people that you can TRUST, who LOVE and
RESPECT your PRIVATE BODY, know what is RIGHT
and WRONG when it comes to playing and helping kids.

WHO CAN YOU TRUST?

A BIG PERSON
who RESPECTS your
PRIVATE BODY.

This could be...
a parent,
a teacher
a school counselor
a bigger sister or brother
a neighbor
a police person
a firefighter
an adult at your
church or synogue
or special group or club.

26

ANOTHER
BIG PERSON who RESPECTS
your PRIVATE BODY.

This could be...
a parent,
a teacher
a school counselor
a bigger sister or brother
a neighbor
a police person
a firefighter
an adult at your
church or synogue
or special group or club.

KEEP TELLING BIG PEOPLE
UNTIL SOMEONE LISTENS AND HELPS.

Remember.

A big person, that you should be able to trust,
that tells you to keep secrets about
touching, CANNOT BE TRUSTED.

Even if...

They give you candy
or toys
or money
or take you to awesome places
that you really want to go...
They can't be trusted.
It is wrong to try to trick or bribe you to
keep a secret about touching.

Remember.

There are KNOW tiny secrets
to keep with a big person who doesn't know right from
wrong when it comes to BEING AROUND KIDS
AND TOUCHING.

Even if...

A big person tries to scare you...
threatens to hurt you...
or says
NOBODY WILL BELIEVE YOU.

Remember.

TELL ANOTHER BIG PERSON
that you can trust.

RIGHT AWAY. TELL THEM EVERYTHING.
THEY WILL BELIEVE YOU.

Remember.

Bad people will try to make you be quiet.
Bad people will want you to feel ashamed.
DON'T be quiet and DON'T be ashamed.
You did NOTHING wrong and YOU are not bad.

There are kNOw secrets or tickles
or games that a bad person
wants to do to your private
places that is EVER your fault.

Tell. Tell right away
and be brave.
The good big people who love you
and care about you
will help you
and will be very proud of you
that you told them what happened.

You won't be a little kid forever.
Soon, you'll be big enough to say in a
very big voice...
NO!
THIS IS MY BODY AND IT IS PRIVATE.

You'll be bigger and brave...and very smart. And safe.
You'll watch for signs and you'll know who you can trust
and who to tell. Your friends will be bigger, too.
They can help and they can tell, too.
You'll be an unstoppable team of very brave kids!

As you see...we all started here.
New and small.

And we needed so many things.
Love and warmth and safety.

But now...you're bigger and...

Do you know that
you are WONDERFULLY MADE?
You are brave, smart and
oh so unique!

Be proud of all those
cute freckles, those cool glasses
those funky braids!

Those missing teeth!

Look in the mirror
and love
who you see
every day
and say...

There are
kNOw tiny
SECRETS
when it comes to
MY BODY...

38

...And there never will be.

40

Made in the USA
Columbia, SC
18 January 2018